D1199220

Gross History

Gross FACTS About the Roman Empire

BY MIRA VONNE

CAPSTONE PRESS
a capstone imprint

Blazers Books are published by Capstone Press,
1710 Roe Crest Drive, North Mankato, Minnesota 56003
www.mycapstone.com

Copyright © 2017 by Capstone Press, a Capstone imprint. All rights reserved. No part of this
publication may be reproduced in whole or in part, or stored in a retrieval system, or transmitted
in any form or by any means, electronic, mechanical, photocopying, recording, or otherwise,
without written permission of the publisher.

Library of Congress Cataloging-in-Publication Data
Names: Vonne, Mira, author.
Title: Gross facts about the Roman Empire / by Mira Vonne.
Description: North Mankato, Minnesota : Capstone Press, [2016] | Series:
    Blazers. Gross history | Includes bibliographical references and index.
Identifiers: LCCN 2016032451 (print) | LCCN 2016033190 (ebook) | ISBN
    9781515741565 (library binding) | ISBN 9781515741732 (pbk.) | ISBN
    9781515741794 (eBook PDF)
Subjects: LCSH: Rome—Social life and customs—Juvenile literature. |
    Rome—Social conditions—Juvenile literature.
Classification: LCC DG78 .V65 2016 (print) | LCC DG78 (ebook) | DDC
    937/.06—dc23
LC record available at https://lccn.loc.gov/2016032451

Editorial Credits
Mandy Robbins, editor; Philippa Jenkins, designer; Wanda Winch, media researcher;
Steve Walker, production specialist

Photo Credits
Alamy: Lanmas, 5 (top); Bridgeman Images: © Look and Learn/Private Collection/Severino
Baraldi, 25, © Bonhams, London, UK/Private Collection/Modesto Faustini, 7, © Historic England/
Private Collection/Judith Dobie, 9, Archives Charmet/Bibliotheque des Arts Decoratifs, Paris,
France/Antonio Niccolini, 23, Archives Charmet/Private Collection/Italian School, 18-19, J. Paul
Getty Museum, Los Angeles, USA/Roberto Bompiani, 17; Capstone, 5 (map); Getty Images: DEA
Picture Library, 13; Johnny Shumate, 29; Newscom: akg-images/Peter Connolly, 11; North Wind
Picture Archives, 15, Gerry Embleton, 21; Shutterstock: irin-k, fly design, Milan M, color splotch
design, monkeystock, grunge drip design, Protasov AN, weevil, lice, parasites, Spectral-Design,
28; SuperStock: iberphoto, 27; Thinkstock: Photos.com, cover

Essential content terms are **bold** and are defined on the page where they first appear.

Printed and bound in China

9941S17RRD

TABLE OF CONTENTS

Filthy Streets

The Roman **Empire** once ruled all the lands around the Mediterranean Sea. **Ancient** Romans had many tools that helped make their lives easier. But other parts of Roman life were dirty, gross, or even deadly.

empire—a large area ruled by a powerful leader

ancient—belonging to the very distant past and no longer in existence

4

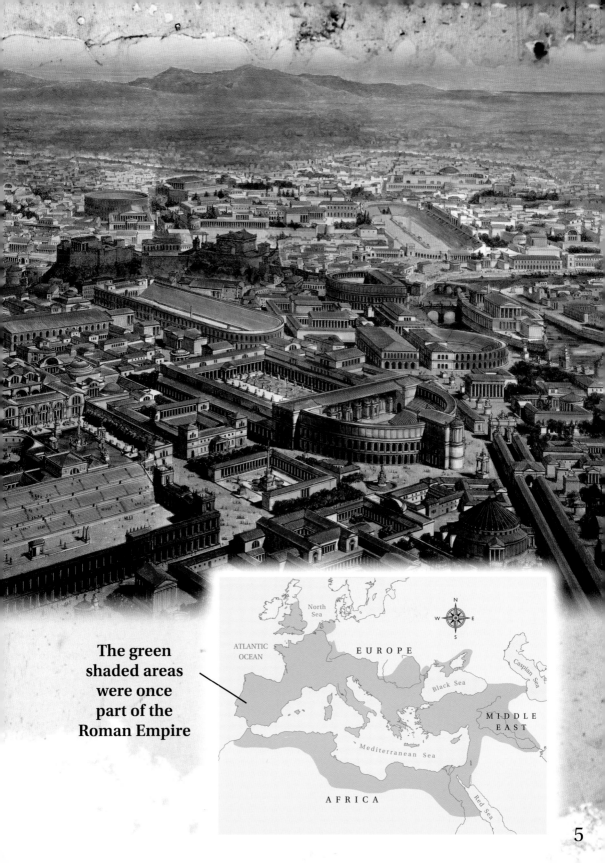

The green shaded areas were once part of the Roman Empire

North Sea

ATLANTIC OCEAN

EUROPE

Caspian Sea

Black Sea

MIDDLE EAST

Mediterranean Sea

AFRICA

Red Sea

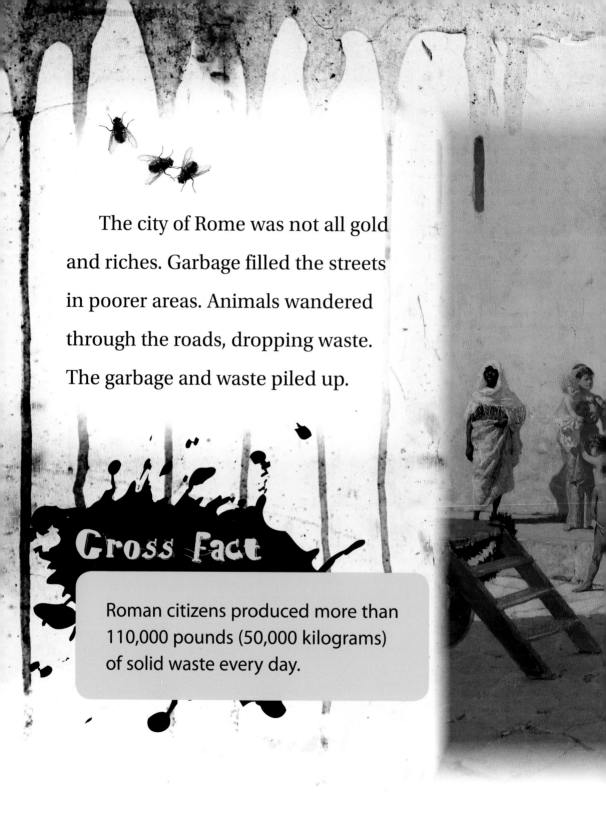

The city of Rome was not all gold and riches. Garbage filled the streets in poorer areas. Animals wandered through the roads, dropping waste. The garbage and waste piled up.

Gross Fact

Roman citizens produced more than 110,000 pounds (50,000 kilograms) of solid waste every day.

Animals were **butchered** in the street for their meat. The remains were tossed into the sewer. Rainwater washed the waste from the sewers into the Tiber River. The awful smell of rotting flesh stayed behind.

butcher—to cut up raw meat

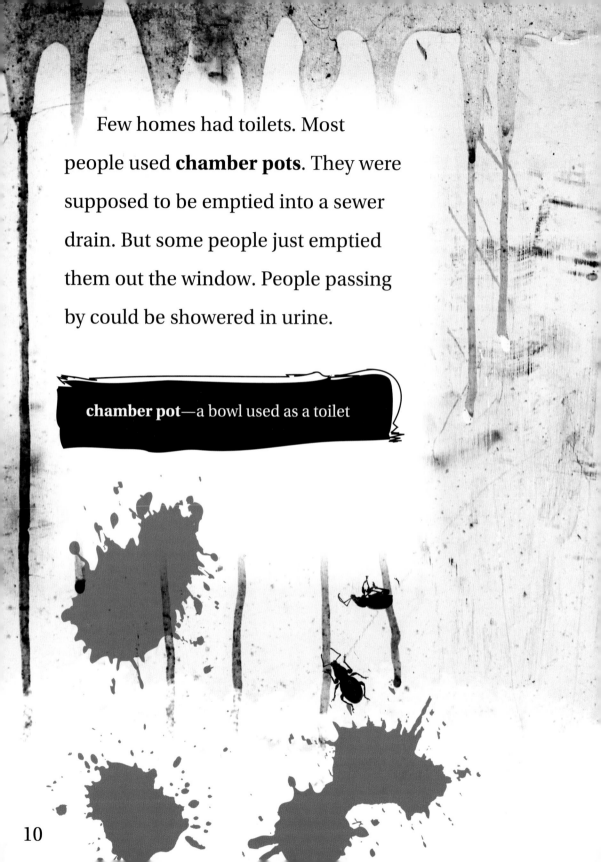

Few homes had toilets. Most people used **chamber pots**. They were supposed to be emptied into a sewer drain. But some people just emptied them out the window. People passing by could be showered in urine.

chamber pot—a bowl used as a toilet

There were laws against throwing waste out the window. However, many people ignored them. The city hired workers to keep the streets clean. But the **sewage** always seemed to build up again.

sewage—human waste that is today carried away in sewers and drains

Citizens and Slaves

Wealthy Romans bought and sold goods throughout the empire. This included people. For many enslaved people, life was horrible. Some owners **branded** or tattooed their slaves' faces. Others were bound with heavy chains.

brand—to mark the skin with a hot iron, sometimes as a mark of disgrace

Cross Fact

Some enslaved people killed their babies at birth rather than let them become slaves.

Gross Grub

Rich Romans threw fancy dinner parties. Hosts served strange food such as tongue and brains. Sometimes birds were stuffed with mice. Guests ate all parts of the bird except its beak.

Gross Fact

Cooking with garum was a popular practice. This sauce was made from aged fish heads, fins, and guts.

Keeping Clean

Romans didn't have soap to wash clothes. Instead, laundry workers set out pots on the street. Roman men would relieve themselves into these pots. Dirty clothes were then soaked and scrubbed in huge tubs of urine.

19

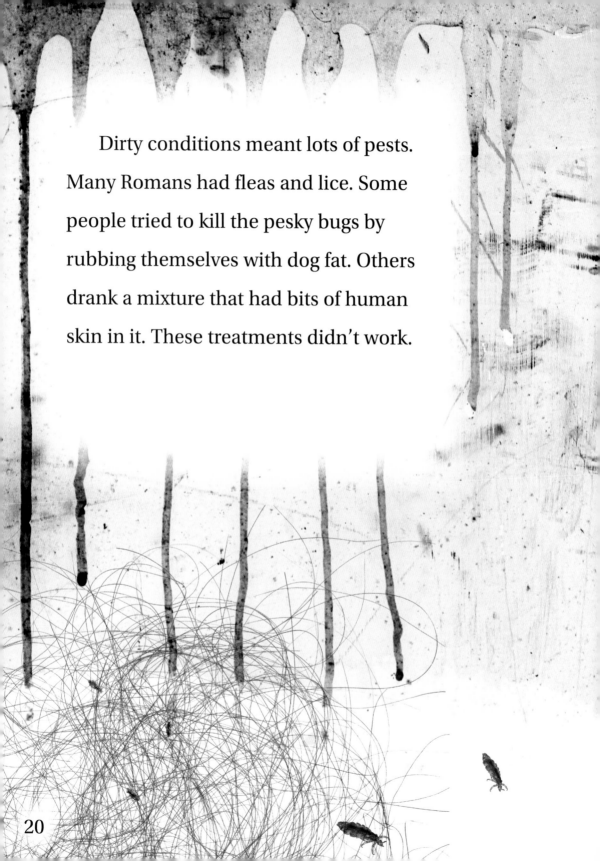

Dirty conditions meant lots of pests. Many Romans had fleas and lice. Some people tried to kill the pesky bugs by rubbing themselves with dog fat. Others drank a mixture that had bits of human skin in it. These treatments didn't work.

Deadly Sports

Romans packed into **arenas** to watch deadly games. **Gladiators** fought one another or wild animals such as rhinos and bears. Many animals were killed during the battles. Their bodies were thrown into the Tiber River.

arena—a large area in which sports, entertainment, and other public events are held

gladiator—a man trained to fight with weapons against other men or wild animals in an arena

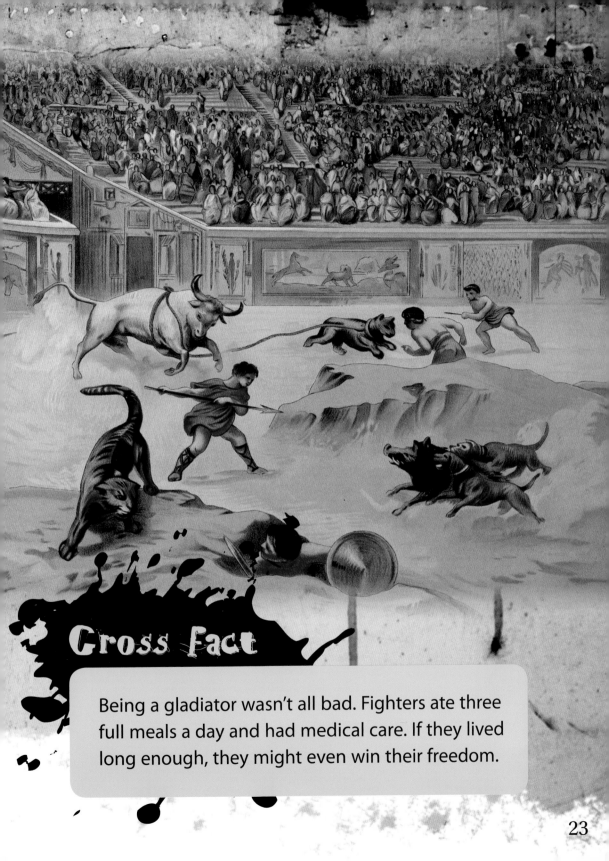

Gross Fact

Being a gladiator wasn't all bad. Fighters ate three full meals a day and had medical care. If they lived long enough, they might even win their freedom.

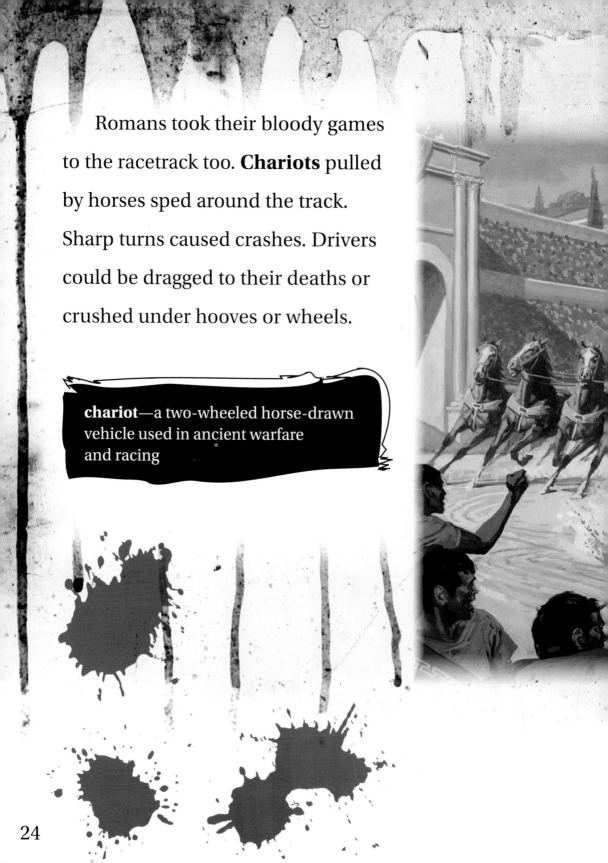

Romans took their bloody games to the racetrack too. **Chariots** pulled by horses sped around the track. Sharp turns caused crashes. Drivers could be dragged to their deaths or crushed under hooves or wheels.

chariot—a two-wheeled horse-drawn vehicle used in ancient warfare and racing

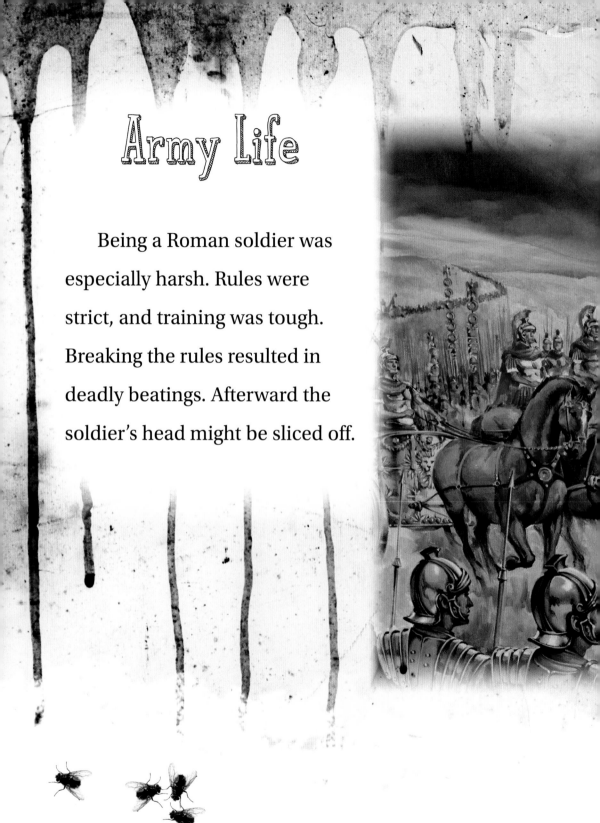

Army Life

Being a Roman soldier was especially harsh. Rules were strict, and training was tough. Breaking the rules resulted in deadly beatings. Afterward the soldier's head might be sliced off.

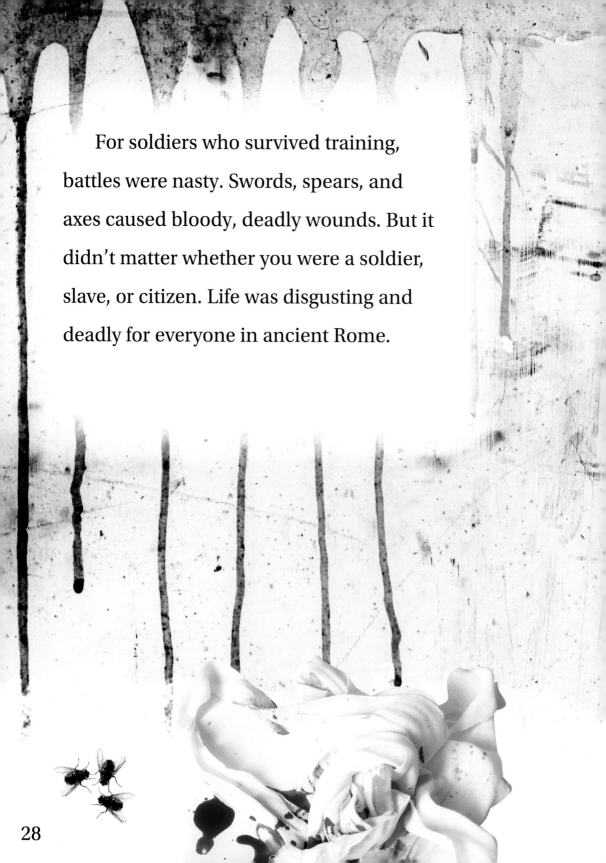

For soldiers who survived training, battles were nasty. Swords, spears, and axes caused bloody, deadly wounds. But it didn't matter whether you were a soldier, slave, or citizen. Life was disgusting and deadly for everyone in ancient Rome.

Glossary

ancient (AIN-chent)—belonging to the very distant past and no longer in existence

arena (uh-REE-nuh)—a large area in which sports, entertainment, and other public events are held

brand (BRAND)—to mark the skin with a hot iron, sometimes as a mark of disgrace

butcher (BU-chur)—to cut up raw meat

chamber pot (CHAME-bur POT)—a bowl used as a toilet

chariot (CHAIR-ee-ut)—a two-wheeled horse-drawn vehicle used in ancient warfare and racing

empire (EM-pire)—a large area ruled by a powerful leader

gladiator (GLAD-ee-AY-tur)—a man trained to fight with weapons against other men or wild animals in an arena

sewage (SOO-uhj)—human waste that is today carried away in sewers and drains

sewer (SUE-er)—an underground pipe for carrying off drainage water and waste matter

Read More

Bingham, Jane. E*xplore!: Romans*. Explore. New York: Wayland, 2017.

Dubois, Muriel L. *Ancient Rome: A Mighty Empire*. Great Civilizations. North Mankato, Minn.: Capstone Press, 2012.

Ganeri, Anita. *How to Live Like a Roman Gladiator*. How to Live Like... Minneapolis: Hungry Tomato, 2015.

Internet Sites

FactHound offers a safe, fun way to find Internet sites related to this book. All of the sites on FactHound have been researched by our staff.

Here's all you do:

Visit *www.facthound.com*

Type in this code: 9781515741565

 Check out projects, games and lots more at
www.capstonekids.com

Critical Thinking Using the Common Core

- The details in this book are gross. What other words can you use to describe the Roman Empire? (Key Ideas and Details)

- How do the images add information about the Roman Empire? Describe some of these images. (Craft and Structure)

- Consider how people lived in the Roman Empire. Would you want to live during this time? Why or why not? (Integration of Knowledge and Ideas)

Index